WHY BLACK AND BROWN KIDS DON'T ICE SKATE

—

Joel Savary, Author and founder of Diversify Ice Foundation

A discourse on the disparities of race in figure skating.

Library of Congress Control Number: 2020900418

ISBN 9781672888028

Ebook ISBN 9780578633268

Cover design by Cary Michaels

WHY BLACK AND BROWN KIDS DON'T ICE SKATE

A discourse on the state of figure skating, as it pertains to race, and how we can make it more reflective of America's racial and cultural diversity.

About the Author

Joel Savary is the founder of Diversify Ice Foundation, a non-profit aimed to diversify the sport of figure skating by cultivating skaters of color. In his new book, "Why Black and Brown Kids Don't Ice Skate," Joel outlines many of the issues plaguing the sport and provides strategies for infusing diversity to reinvigorate the sport overall.

Mr. Savary is also a National and International figure skating coach in the Washington, D.C area. He has performed on a number of national and international ice-skating shows, such as Disney on Ice. Today he coaches skaters of all ages and ability in the greater Washington D.C. area.

Mr. Savary is most noted for his work with his younger brother, Emmanuel Savary, who has won the U.S. Jr. National Championships and several international events. Along with Emmanuel's head coaches, he has helped to cultivate his brother to be a competitive Team USA athlete who has now reached the Senior Men's Championship level.

In Recognition

To my parents who sacrificed their lives in helping my brother and I achieve our dreams in figure skating. They never gave up on us, even if the racial disparities in the sport meant the odds were against us. I love you for encouraging us even when the world and the sport may not have always been kind.

To my brothers, Johnathan and Emmanuel, who didn't ridicule me (for long) for joining an unconventional sport. Your support has helped me to continue to make an impact in the sport today.

To the Saunders family for your selflessness in supporting me in this book launch and many of my other personal goals. I could not have done it without you. Also, to the youngest, thank you for being a joy to coach!

To the black and brown kids who want to make something of themselves in ice skating—don't give up! Your time is coming.

Diversify Ice CEO, Joel Savary:
Figure Skating needs to address the race issue head on

Why don't black and brown kids ice skate? You may have wondered why so few people of color take to the ice. Until now, no one has addressed this issue head on. While many historically racially homogenous sports, such as gymnastics, tennis, swimming, and golf, are seeing an increase in diversity of black and brown athletes in recent years, the sport of figure skating has remained monochromatic. In many areas, the sport has even taken steps backwards in the representation and participation of Black and Brown skaters nationally and internationally. While figure skating in America is undergoing significant challenges in popularity and ratings, in recent years, an even greater challenge is the issue of race in the sport. Many of these issues would be improved by fostering diversity among elite athletes in the sport. To date, there hasn't been any concerted effort to diversify figure skating of elite black and brown kids through the figure skating governance. With America's demographic rapidly changing, figure skating in America needs to adapt and cultivate minority participation in order to survive.

Table of Contents

Preface

Imagine: a young, sun-kissed, black boy from Miami enters a frigid ice rink for the first time. Inside, a white sheet of ice, the size of a football field, absorbs his reflection. White skates attached to metallic blades hovers above the ice and revolves as fast as a basketball rotating on his finger. White faces peer back at him with a hint of suspicion—low, confused murmurs asking, "What is that boy doing here?"

I don't have to imagine this story, because this is my story. I've lived and observed these experiences as a black boy in the skating world. Luckily, I was one of the few minorities who didn't let the initial negative interaction deter me from coming back and enjoying the sport I love. Unfortunately, undesirable social experiences only hit the surface of why many kids of color decide not to participate in ice skating as a sport.

In this book, I hope to shed light on some of the most pervasive racial issues in skating that are rarely spoken about. The minorities that continue in figure skating are often worn down by the time-honored systems that reward conformity and impede diversity. For example, figure skating's subjective judging requires competitive skaters to assimilate to a contrived ideal look, in order to receive positive presentation and program component scores. This is unrealistic for people of color, so they are rarely awarded and celebrated for their cultural differences and unique style.

"Every time you state what you want or believe, you're the first to hear it. It's a message to both you and others about what you think is possible. Don't put a ceiling on yourself."

– Oprah Winfrey

THE STORY: Autobiographical Discourse on Racial Disparities

CHAPTER 1

"This sport is so expensive"

My parents, immigrants from Jamaica, were avid Olympic fans and instilled that love in their American-born kids. As a family, we watched both the Summer and Winter Olympics, which alternated every two years. Although we watched most events, the events we couldn't miss were track and field, gymnastics, tennis, and, above all, ice skating. Although my parents had their favorites, I typically rooted for the underdog. Whenever the underdog won, my parents used that moment to share with us kids that anything was truly possible if we worked hard, took risks, and believed in ourselves.

My dad, while living in Jamaica, was training to be a track and field star. He was tapped as a talent to train with some of the best athletes in Jamaica, but he turned down the opportunity to instead learn a trade, which was a surer way to support his family financially than the uncertainty of sports. I learned that he regretted that decision, after meeting some of his former classmates. Runners who were not nearly as fast as him, but took that chance, found some success at the national and international levels. I believe this is why he was supportive of all my crazy interests and initiatives, including training to be a gymnast, track and field, and learning tennis. In time, I would develop an interest of pursuing an atypical sport that caught my entire family off-guard, and may have changed the trajectory of our lives forever.

***

It was report card time—the time of year when most fourteen-year-old sons of Jamaican immigrants fear bringing home anything less than straight A's. I knew how important education was to my parents because they did not have the same educational opportunities in Jamaica as I did in America. Although I did not get straight A's that year, I did earn my way on the honor roll, again. This year, everyone who made the honor roll was given a *Winner Circle,* free tear-away tickets and coupons on a circular perforated paper. These tickets had fun activities and products from local vendors such as bowling, pizza, and ice cream.

This year, however, I noticed something new on the Winner Circle Award—A free ticket to ice skating. Who knew ice skating existed in Miami? I didn't. We were in the sunshine state after all. This, I had to see in person!

I begged my mom to take me to the ice rink that Saturday telling her how much "I earned it" because of my good grades. I saw her hesitation at first, but it was free with the ticket, so in the end she promised to take me. I could tell my mom was excited to see the ice rink, as well. The rink was in the nice part of Miami, and it took us about thirty minutes to get there with my mom's heavy right foot. Right next door was an exotic car dealership and we were only a couple of minutes from the beach.

It was a very hot day and I remember bringing a very light windbreaker jacket, which did nothing to keep me warm inside the cold ice rink. However, I was too excited to care about how cold I was. I tried on my first pair of plastic, blue, worn-out, rental figure skates at the Miami Ice Arena. These skates had no ankle support and were likely very dull, but back then, I wouldn't have recognized the difference. I tried doing all of the "tricks" I had seen on TV—spinning, jumping, and dancing across the ice. I was having so much fun gliding and moving across the ice, and it wasn't long before I realized that kids were circled around me, watching and clapping. I felt connected with the ice. A blonde-haired woman approached me and introduced herself as a coach.

She suggested I take lessons to refine my ability, especially after learning that I had taught myself all of these "tricks" in the span of two hours on a public session. While we were leaving the rink, I told my mom that a coach wanted to teach me professionally. She was hesitant at first because of the costs for lessons and ice time, and moreover, she wanted to make sure I was focused more on my education. In the end, however, she agreed that I could skate after school, as long as I completed all my homework.

For the most part, my lessons with my new coach were on public sessions on Saturday mornings. However, as my abilities advanced from simple spins to more advanced double jumps and spins, the dimly-lit public session was not a viable option to continue my training. The public sessions continued to get more crowded and the flashing neon lights could give anyone a seizure, especially while spinning and jumping on blades that measured a quarter of an inch thick.

Within a few months, my coach said that my skating abilities had advanced to a high enough level to train on the freestyle sessions, which were a special ice time designated for "serious skaters" training for competition. This advancement meant I would have to take the city bus after school to reach the ice rink in time for the sessions, because my mom was working and taking night classes. My coach also said that per rink policy, I must use my own skates to be on the freestyle session. She brought my mom and me to the skate shop, which was located inside the ice rink, and pointed out to my parents the type of skates I would need for my skating ability and level.

The figure skates in this shop were upwards of five hundred dollars, even for the low-quality skates. Unfortunately, all of the skates were way too expensive for my family and my mom let her know that we couldn't afford it. Instead, my coach pointed us to a hockey skate shop a few blocks away, which often had used figure skates that they would sell at a bargain.

This skate shop primarily had hockey equipment and only a small selection of ice skates. Surprisingly, they had a pair of brand-new skates that someone had recently returned, which happened to be exactly my size. The skate shop wanted to get rid of them and sold them to us for a much lower price than their value. I believe this was a sign that my journey into the skating world was meant to be.

My mom made the sacrifice to buy the ice skates, which ran at a couple of hundred dollars. Upsettingly, this also meant I couldn't get the latest video game I really wanted. This was the first of many sacrifices I would have to make for my love of skating.

"If I didn't define myself for myself,
I would be crunched into other
people's fantasies for me and
eaten alive."

— Audre Lorde

Chapter 2

"Are those your ice skates?"

I was excited to participate in my first advanced freestyle session after school. I rode the city bus with a big bag, which held my books, school supplies—and ice skates. I got there an hour before my lesson started. While waiting in the bleachers, I watched some of the more advanced ice skaters. I was not sure how the skaters were able to get out of school so early to skate. I soon learned that many of the ice skaters were homeschooled or in a private school that set up a special schedule with the skaters. The atmosphere was very different from the public sessions. I noticed that everyone had on custom leather figure skates, which were polished white for the girls and black for the boys. Instead of the public session music, which consisted of songs heard on the Top 100, this session played mostly classical music for the skaters practicing their routines. All of the typical figure skating music you heard at the Olympics were played—"Beethoven, Carmen, and Swan Lake"—and the ice rink was brightly lit for the freestyle session, so that the skaters could train more effectively. This skating atmosphere was different from practicing in the dark, recreational, public sessions. It was exciting to see all of the skaters jumping, spinning, and falling multiple times to perfect each move.

I was very excited to try my very own ice skates. As I was pulling my skates out of my blue sporty duffle bag, a woman on the ice motioned to me with a look of disdain on her face. She mouthed to me "Are those your skates?" I responded "Yes." She then came off the ice and approached me repeating the question

"Are those your skates?" I responded again in my crackly teenage voice, "Yes." She said, "No they're not; you are trying to take someone's skates." I responded that "these were my skates my mom bought for me." I then saw her rush off the ice to the front office. where she pointed at me while talking to the staff. Although I did not hear that conversation, I can imagine what she said.

I felt very uneasy. I was the only African American kid at the ice rink. My first private freestyle lesson was starting soon, so I laced up my skates and took to the ice with an uncomfortable fear that I would be pulled off — or worse, hauled off in hand cuffs — for her false allegation. I didn't have time to waste. My mom only gave me enough money for one freestyle session, which was twelve dollars for fifty minutes. I pushed the woman to the back of my mind and proceeded to the ice.

I got on the ice and started warming up for my first lesson. When the lady returned to the ice, she noticed I was jumping and spinning in my skates. She then said to me "Oh, I didn't realize—I've never seen you here before." She never apologized for the false accusation. When I looked around me, it was then that it hit me. Because everyone around me was white, it was more practical for this woman to believe that I was someone stealing skates rather than a skater, simply because I was a black boy. At the age of fourteen, that was my first experience understanding being an outsider because of my race and I learned it at an ice rink trying to figure skate.

"What's the world for if you can't make it up the way you want it?"

– Toni Morrison

Chapter 3

"Black people don't ice skate!"

As figure skating became integrated into my weekly routine, I took pride in the work I had accomplished on the ice. I was now completing all of the double jumps, variations of triple jumps, and a variety of spins. So, when my eighth-grade classroom initiated an ice-breaker session asking each student to share what sport they played, I was excited to share my sport. As the teacher went around the room to ask my predominantly Black and Hispanic classmates to share the sport they enjoyed playing the most, it wasn't surprising that each student reeled off similar answers like "I like playing basketball," "I love playing football," and "I'm in track." However, when it was my turn, I told the class

"I like playing ice skating." It was a weird feeling as the words escaped my mouth, maybe from realizing how different my sport was, and even associating the word "play" with "ice skating" did not roll off the tongue correctly because it didn't feel like a game—more like a special activity. There were a few snickers from classmates and then, horrifically, a student shouted, "Black people don't ice skate!" and then another classmate chuckled while saying, "Ice skating is for girls." That instant sense of embarrassment was mortifying. It was hurtful to know that my peers didn't think the sport I was doing was cool.

The teacher calmed the class down, but from that moment I recoiled from sharing about my love for ice skating. When I mentioned this to my parents, they said clearly, "Do not let anyone tell you what you can or cannot do." However, I think the social pressure, from friends that looked like me and from kids that didn't, was too hurtful. Soon enough, ice skating became a secret activity for me, and I hesitated before sharing it with anyone for

fear of the judgement that I may be perceived as feminine or not

culturally connected to people who looked like me.

Photo of Joel in grade school. Photo courtesy of Jennifer Savary (Mother)

Chapter 4

So, you want to be an elite skater?

WHERE TO GET STARTED IF YOU WANT TO TRAIN SERIOUSLY

I was lucky. Although I started skating as a teenager, which is a relatively late age in the sport of figure skating, I was able to learn all of the difficult triple jumps pretty quickly. My coaches in Florida, who realized my ability to learn the difficult jumps, suggested that I train in either Delaware, Colorado Springs, or California (Lake Arrowhead) for the summer. These were the primary skating hubs where serious skaters can train under the auspices of some of the renowned coaches and alongside the most established skaters in America. Skaters from all over the world came to these training sites for the high-level training facilities and coaching staff. I did well in my local south Florida competitions, though there weren't many local male competitors. So I was happy when my family made the sacrifice to drive to Delaware to give me the opportunity to skate among the best (this road trip also doubled as a family vacation).

After just a couple months of training with the elite athletes and coaches, my triples became bigger and more consistent, and my younger brother was also able to get an early experience training at that level. Fortunately, while I was training in the summer skating camp in Delaware, an opportunity opened up for my dad to work as a lead electrical project manager near the Delaware ice rinks. This meant my younger brother and I would be able to stay in Delaware to train alongside the best towards our Olympic goals. What made this move even more exciting was that there were at least two other African American skaters at our rink.

We quickly learned that our move to one of these skating hubs was more common than we originally thought. Many families split just so their child can train with elite coaches, while the rest of the family remained in their home city. Parents often make arrangement for the kid to live with their coach or at a skating host family. Also, families all over America make huge financial commitments to help their children towards their goals. In fact, many families took out a second mortgage to cover the training expenses of their child with the hopes of Olympic stardom. Skating is a gamble, however, with an added element of subjectivity, so these sacrifices dio not always yield stardom.

HANDLING HARDSHIPS

During my skating career, my mother suffered a stroke, and the financial burden became increasingly heavy for my family, to the point where my brother and I no longer could afford lessons from our elite coaches. This family crisis could have prevented my brother and I from ever skating at an elite level again. However, I picked up several odd jobs to help my family, and I transitioned to helping my brother in his training. Many days, we could only afford one elite freestyle practice session or one public session, while our competitors were skating at least three sessions a day. To this day, I remember creating a detailed training schedule to utilize every minute of the hour we had on the session. We crammed three practice sessions into one, so he could be on par with his competitors. Even with our limited training time, we pushed the envelope. He was completing difficult triple-triple jumps at the age of nine. Instead of training in the elite gym and ballet skating facilities, we were relegated to using the gym in our apartment. We understood the importance of dedication early on, even through adversity, to find success.

After several months, my mom's health improved, and we were able to resume my brother's lessons with his head coaches. From that point on, I remained an integral part of my brother's training team and was fortunate to work alongside some of his head coaches in Delaware, who are known to be some of the best coaches in the world.

Chapter 5

Envisioning a more diverse sport

The hardships that I endured as a skater and witnessed as my brother's coach made me realize that something needed to be done to help minority kids in figure skating. I knew that my family couldn't have been the only skating family that endured these hardships. The more I spoke with other minority skaters, the more I heard patterns of frustrations about the sport we loved. The consistent frustrations I heard from other families included the outrageous costs, lack of support, confusing information, lack of community, and suppression of identity and culture. I was able to crystalize the experiences I had and find many similarities in the difficulties that minorities, at various levels, experienced in figure skating. The financial barrier is only one small part of the issue for the lack of diversity in figure skating.

This prompted me to start the Diversify Ice Foundation. My goal was to tackle all the issues that contributes to a lack of diversity at the elite levels of figure skating. To accomplish this, we first needed to raise awareness of ice skating as a viable option in communities of color. Then, we needed to increase minority participation at every level. I was fortunate that I was able to pull together a talented team that connected to the mission to be on my board. In some of our earlier efforts, we tried new marketing techniques to attract more people of color. We realized that the methods used nationally does little to attract people of color to skating. We found success in our events and attracted more skaters to come back for private and group lessons.

To reach the younger crowd, I visited schools with predominately African American and Latino students to sell them on the joys of figure skating. This was critically important for me, recognizing that I got my start to ice skating through school. Now when kids, and even adults, mentioned to me that "Black and Brown kids don't ice skate," I was able to prove them wrong.

Since starting the Diversify Ice Foundation over three years ago, a number of minority skaters, parents, and coaches have reached out to the foundation, expressing their frustrations with being left out of the equation in figure skating. These qualms include skaters of color being overlooked for parts in shows, not scored fairly in competitions (though this sentiment is felt from many skaters, regardless of race), and feeling their coaches are holding them back from progressing. Parents and coaches alike have expressed concern about the lack of a support system needed to keep their kids interested in the sport long-term. While these issues may be shared by all, there is longstanding history of unfair treatment of minorities by the figure skating governance, coaches and judges. For example, Mabel Fairbanks who was denied access to skate and later prevented from competing because she was a person of color. In addition, Debi Thomas who repeatedly scored lower than her competitors, even though she had more difficult skating skills and stronger performances. As a result of these and other common experiences, minorities often have a lack of trust in the figure skating system. Much needs to be done to mend these wounds.

Chapter 6

Sacrifices for Success in Skating

In general, the sacrifices to excel in the sport go beyond on-ice training—it's a lifestyle. Managing a healthy weight and diet, attaining enough sleep daily, maintaining a good workout regimen off the ice, positive reinforcement from coaches and training team, incorporating elements of dance and ballet, and emphasis on good technique for consistency and advancement of jumps and spins are just some of the lifestyle practices that need to be incorporated for success. At an elite level, adopting these lifestyle practices can mean making certain sacrifices that kids may not be used to. For example, skaters may not always be able to hang out with school friends, have that extra slice of cake ahead of a competition, or make time for additional fun activities that may conflict with their training schedule. Some of these examples may seem extreme but, they often have real consequences. What may appear to be a trivial pound or two gained before a competition, can affect a skater's ability to land their jumps. Elite skaters often keep a consistent weight because any changes in their body can throw off jumps, spins and even their flow on the ice.

On top of these lifestyle practices needed for all skaters, minority skaters must also have an increase aptitude for mental toughness. As a coach, one of my students said she felt alone at many competitions. She mentioned there were no other skaters who looked like her and other skaters did not seem open to being friends. While I provided her the support she needed at the time and reinforced confidence in her performance, we were the only people of color at the rink and were treated that way. Competition staff immediately assumed I was the skater's parent as opposed to her coach. Other coaches of color have shared similar stories. On another occasion, one of my students and I were instantly told at the door that the rink was not open for public sessions that day, without asking what we were there for. Although I repeatedly mentioned our intention to skate on a freestyle session, the staff continued to assume we were there to skate on a public session.

To find success in the sport, a skater must have the backing of their family. This family support is important, in part, because of the large financial investment that is required. In addition, the social pressures for minorities to participate in "black activities" instead of a predominately white sport like ice skating can impact their retention in the sport. I remember a father of a very talented black boy, who did not approve of him ice skating because he felt it was too effeminate, and eventually the boy quit to participate in school team sports. When I think of this story, I feel so grateful for my dad who has supported me even though he did not understand my fascination with this sport.

Black and Brown skaters share the same challenges and the same sacrifices as every other skater. However, these challenges are compounded by the racial disparities in the sport. It is often said within the black and brown community that to just to be recognized, you must be twice as good as your white counterparts. Through the examples of figure skating legends who broke barriers, and for many of the current elite minority skaters, that sentiment rings true.

Historically, if you want to train with the best coaches and skaters in the world, there are three primary major skating hubs you should explore. While there are other rinks across America that have created champions in the past, these skating hubs have a track record of consistently developing champions. As shown in the table below, ice rinks are usually located in predominately white affluent neighborhoods, respective to the neighboring towns. Also, if a skater of color wants to take skating seriously and train at some of the best skating centers, they will need to move to towns where they are an overwhelming minority. This is a large sacrifice on many skaters and an even bigger sacrifice on the families.

DMV Local Rinks				*2017 Census Data
Ice Rinks	City/ State	Zip Code	Median Income of town	Demographic
Wheaton Ice rink	Wheaton, MD	20902	87,244	46.0% White, 18.8% Black
Fairfax Ice Arena	Fairfax, VA	22031	110,341	63.8% White, 7% Black
Bowie Ice rink	Bowie, MD	20716	96,492	66.7% Black, 28.0% White
Fort Dupont Ice rink	SE Washington, DC	20019	35,482	95.8% Black, 2.1% White

Cabin John Ice rink	Rockville, MD	20852	94,378	68.8% White, 9.4% Black
Gardens Ice House	Laurel, MD	20702	N/A	
Competitive Training Hubs				
Colorado World Arena	Colorado Springs, CO	80906	62,374	88.1% White, 5.5% Black
UD Ice Arena	Newark, DE	19716		81.3% White, 12.9% Black
East West Ice Palace	Artesia, CA	90701	62,863	38.6% White, 5.5% Black

As a study, I also did analysis on ice rinks in the D.C.,

Maryland, Virginia (DMV). While the majority of ice rinks were

located in predominantly affluent white neighborhoods, two ice

rinks were located in black neighborhoods. To no surprise, these

rinks did have more skaters of color on the ice. Surprisingly

however, the Diversify Ice Foundation reached out to families in

these minority communities about participating in ice skating, but many of the families didn't even know the ice rink was open to the public. In addition, initial thoughts from families in the community were that ice rinks were only open in the winter and that the cost to skate would be too expensive.

Joe

l taking a class with Legendary Coach, Frank Carroll. Photo courtesy of Joel Savary

Chapter 7

Diversity we have seen, so far

SKATERS OF COLOR EXIST

As a skater in Delaware, I was happy to see a couple of African American female skaters on the ice. Both African Americans at this rink were very talented and powerful skaters. I wondered why I hadn't seen them on TV or on the senior elite national stage. They were landing all of the same triple jumps that the other American skaters were doing on television, yet I wouldn't even know that other black and brown skaters existed until I came to this rink. Surprisingly, these skaters were at the senior elite level, but just weren't televised at the extent of other non-black and brown skaters. At the National championships,

usually the top twelve figure skaters from the short program are

televised. Although many of these skaters performed well, they did

not receive high presentation scores as others, leaving them below

the top twelve for television. In addition, the successes of skaters at

the lower intermediate and novice levels are often showcased on

television early on in their career and put on a trajectory of

success. However, we haven't been given the opportunity to watch

minority skaters develop through the ranks publicly on television

at that same level. For example, I remember meeting a very

talented skater of color who was landing all of the difficult triple

jumps as a kid. However, when she grew nearly four inches one

summer during her Junior competitive year, she lost the ability to

land any of these critical jumps and eventually decided to retire.

The world will never have a chance to see her talent or know her

name.

With the popularity of figure skating dwindling in the United States, televised skating time is limited. Spotlights on favorites and featured stories on popular skaters could impact that number and which skater receives the most T.V. time. I initially thought, "What a missed opportunity for the television network, and for the skating community, by not showcasing whatever diversity exists in American skaters regardless of placement. Seeing someone who looks different, like skaters of color, would bring in more viewers, revenue, and diversity." It might be beneficial to at least show the highlights of the remaining skaters, such as one jump or one spin from each skater, so viewers can see all the skaters that made it to this point.

After the end of my competitive journey, I sought out opportunities to make a career out of figure skating in shows. I was quickly picked up for international traveling shows for my ability

to perform the elements they wanted, however there were no real

opportunities for a black man of a darker complexion to play the

large roles, which paid more, no matter what their abilities were.

At the time, the only prince and princess movies featured on

Disney were those of white men or men of light skin complexion.

Attaining these roles required you to look the part more than your

skill and ability. While certain skaters may be able to perform the

difficult triple jumps, they may lose the lead role to someone who

physically looks more the part. Therefore, it was unrealistic for

minorities to attain a role as a lead. There were no lead

protagonists of color in the movies, which meant there would be no

leads of color in the associated ice-skating shows. Today, we see

great changes in the landscape of prince and princess movies on

Disney, which has also allowed for opportunities for skaters of

color in more modern Disney Ice shows, such as the Princess and the Frog. More recent shows like Universoul Circus, a black owned circus, developed ice skating shows which highlighted minority skaters and performers.

PEOPLE OF COLOR DO NOT WATCH SKATING

The figure skating governance has collected demographics of their fan profile and published it publicly on the USFSA website highlighting only two percent of viewers being African American and one percent was Native American. Both are an overwhelming minority in comparison to the seventy-three percent Caucasians and eighteen percent Asians that watch the sport. The demographic of viewers is an indication of the dismal feedback loop we can expect from minority participation in the sport. However, the skating governance does not appear to collect or provide demographic statistics of figure skaters and their membership. It would be beneficial to the governance board to capture statistics of skater membership at all levels, so that they can better target and address the racial disparities in the sport. Although, US Figure skating collects and produces a report on skating membership by age, gender, and membership count, there is no data provided on the race of these skaters.

BLACK MUSIC IN SKATING

When we first moved to Delaware, one of the two African American girls skated to music that had shades of African culture. It was very cool and different from music you would see in televised figure skating. However, I wondered what a culturally conservative judging panel, which is almost always fully represented by older white people, would think of this music. Would they understand the composition or appreciate the stylistic difference of movements that's required to express this piece? Would figure skating judges, who are mostly used to seeing skaters skate to classical music, allow for something different in the sport of figure skating? Unfortunately, I learned after watching many qualifying competitions in real time that the judges were not usually receptive to unconventional skating music choices, regardless of who is skating to it. Judges often hinted to skaters in their after-program evaluations that they should pick something more conventional to be taken seriously. Would Black and Brown skaters have to code-switch, changing the way they express themselves when they are around people with different racial and ethnic backgrounds, by skating to a piece of music that doesn't fully resonate with their soul, in order to be accepted and progress to the next levels? The abysmal results of skaters deviating from the perceived skating norms speak for itself. It would be amazing to hear music choices that expand from the usual Swan Lake to pieces from Aretha Franklin, Beyoncé, Rihanna, Marvin Gaye, Kendrick Lamar, and Michael Jackson, just to name a few. Just think how amazing it would be to see these pieces come to life on the national and international stage from skaters of color.

WHAT ABOUT ASIAN-AMERICAN SKATERS?

While I was training in several high-performance training facilities, there was no shortage of Asian-American figure skaters. I always wondered why was it that figure skating flourished in Asian-American culture, but not in African American culture? From the popularity of Olympic medalist Michelle Kwan and Kristi Yamaguchi, we have seen great success in Asian-Americans in figure skating, but not in African Americans. For one, figure skating is popular in the East, from China to Japan. These countries have the infrastructure to build and maintain high-performing ice rinks, attracting figure skaters into the sport within their country. Many of these skaters are also able to train abroad at high level facilities in North America. In addition, countries like Japan and China have taken figure skating programs very seriously. In fact, they have developed world-class skaters at the Olympics and other international competitions.

When international figure skating competitions are televised in the United States and abroad, the impact to inspire viewers is really powerful. For example, Asian-Americans can immediately watch nearly any international figure skating event and see someone that looks like them and may have cultural references that sends a message that figure skating is acceptable and cool for their culture.

If we are to follow the same lineage back to countries in Africa, we may not see the same infrastructure for building and upkeeping competitive training facilities. It is unlikely to find figure skating rinks devoted to competitive figure skating throughout countries in Africa. Although recreational ice rinks may exist in some countries in Africa, they are usually smaller and not standard training size. What's more, African nations do not attract high-level figure skating coaches, and you will not see their participation in international figure skating events. These countries do not have figure skating teams that are part of the International Skating Union (ISU), the international governing body for competitive ice-skating disciplines, including figure skating, synchronized skating, speed skating, and short track speed skating. Unfortunately, the absence of racial ties makes it difficult for minorities to connect with the sport domestically and internationally.

In 1988, U.S. figure skating sent its first African American skater to the Winter Olympics—no other U.S. skater of color has qualified for either the World Championships or the Winter Olympics in figure skating since. If you've followed skating over the years, you probably remember one African American figure skating talent, Debi Thomas, who skyrocketed to the World and Olympic scene. She was everything the figure skating world loved to see in an African American skater. She skated to recognizable music such as Carmen, by French Composer Georges Bizet, which was the same music as her rival Katarina Witt from East Germany. This rivalry was so important, they called this event the "Battle of the Carmens."

DANIEL JANIN/AFP/GETTY IMAGES, DAVID MADISON/GETTY IMAGES / NBC OLYMPICS

Debi was also well-spoken and very talented. She planned a much more technically difficult program with the very challenging triple-triple jump combination and even a triple loop, both of which Katarina didn't even dare to attempt at the Olympics. Although, Debi did not complete the more difficult moves perfectly, she stayed on her feet. Unfortunately, minor errors on her most difficult moves made her finish in third place, while Katarina's routine, which was technically less difficult, but relatively clean, was crowned with the gold medal.

Surya Bonaly, a French skater of color, was also no stranger to the unfairness of the judging system. She was a very athletic skater that completed the difficult triple-triple combinations and attempted the four revolution quadruple jumps in competition. She also surprised the audience by performing the backflip and landing it on one foot. This backflip was deemed illegal by skating rules. In the 1992 Olympics, she skated a program which included a quadruple toe attempt, which many believe meant she poised to take a medal, especially after the favorites, Kristi Yamaguchi and Nancy Kerrigan, faltered. However, she placed sixth in the long program and fifth overall.

Today, France continues to produce skaters of color at the elite level of figure skating.

Skaters of color that may watch these events and see the disparity in the judging system between skaters of color from their white counterpart may not want to partake in figure skating. A sport that is already so subjective may not cater to people that do not look like everyone else. Black and Brown kids, for that reason, may prefer to participate in sports where there is a clear and transparent winner—non-subjective sports where winning means you either scored the most points or reached the finish line first. Athletes of color have thrived in these more objective sports, such as basketball, football, and is starting to see success in golf and tennis.

Figure skating in America has come from a painful past when it comes to race. Many of the painful stories and images that are not often spoken about widely helped shaped the face of what figure skating looks like today. However, figure skating also has another side to it, where minority figure skaters dared to overcome the racial disparities, challenge the system, and push the envelope on what was technically and artistically acceptable in what is a very white and conservative sport.

One of the earliest and most telling examples of figure skating's tainted past is demonstrated in Mabel Fairbanks' story. Christopher Reed of The Guardian shares how Mabel's efforts to enter a local ice rink were rejected because of her color. She was persistent to skate and was relegated to practice at a makeshift ice rink in her home. He shares that the manager of the public rink noticed her persistence and finally let her into the ice rink. Reed highlights that Mabel was not allowed into the U.S. Olympic trials or any competitive figure skating events. She later became a coach and worked with skaters such as Atoy Wilson, the first black skater to win a U.S. title, and Pairs champions Tai Babilonia and Randy Gardner.

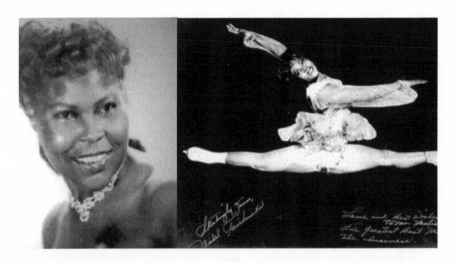

Mabel Fairbanks, Images from <u>Uchenna Edeh</u> (Kentake Page)

Minorities that matriculate to the elite levels of competitive skating often endure discrimination at some point in their skating journey. Encyclopedia Online highlights some examples of Discrimination that Olympian Debi Thomas encountered. According to Encyclopedia.com, "Debi experienced discrimination both overt and subtle. On one occasion, the family returned home from a competition to find a cross burning on their lawn. In addition, judges often gave better marks to Thomas's competitors who had not attempted the technically difficult jumps that Thomas landed so flawlessly."

One of the more popular instances of racial disparity in the sport of figure skating was popularized by the demonizing of black French skater, Surya Bonaly. There were blatant instances where Surya out skated her competitors, but she was still scored lower than skaters who made more errors. One of these examples was at

the 1995 World Championships, where Surya lost by a very small

margin behind Lu Chen of China. In the Sports Illustrated

interview with renowned coach of National Champion Michelle

Kwan, U.S. Frank Carroll stated:

> ``I'm genuinely fond of Surya, but they'd take Chen
> Lu because
> there's just too much bad rap, too much bad
> publicity, too much
> bad talk about Surya that's gone by," says Michelle
> Kwan's coach,
> Frank Carroll, one of Bonaly's sometime mentors.
> ``And, you know,
> it's always the but that does her in: `Surya's a great
> jumper,
> but. . . .' `Surya is a good skater who jumps well,
> but. . . .'
> With Chen Lu, it's just, `She's a beautiful skater.' "

Surya was also demonized for performing an illegal

backflip, landing on one leg, in her competitive practices and

performances. Liz Tims highlights in her article *I, Surya* the harsh

criticisms from judges of something as trivial as her practice costume. Liz states: "In the *Losers* episode, white judge Vanessa Riley criticized one of Bonaly's practice outfits, stating that it was 'more like a court jester. I think that something smart and dignified would have been more appropriate.'"

THE SPORT IS CHANGING

The sport is making strides, in recent years, to address the biased judging and the opaque system of scoring the technical portion of the program, which is made up of jumps and spins and other required elements. For one, the new International Judging System (IJS) uses a base point system for each element performed. However, the performance score and the grade of execution

(GOE), a measurement of the quality of each element performed, is still subjective, although a tiered system is used. This new judging system was in response to a judging scandal at the 2002 Winter Olympics. The previous system was the 6.0 scoring system, where judges evaluated the skater based on a perfect 6.0 score for technical and artistry, which was even more subjective. Figure skating's tainted skating past, marred in scandals, and unfair judging has certainly given a negative view of the sport, which has impacted its popularity. We can hope that with more transparency in judging there will be more opportunities for minority skaters to find success in figure skating.

"Never be limited by other people's limited imaginations."

– Dr. Mae Jamison

Chapter 8

Where do we go from here?

It was like déjà vu, walking into a predominately Black and Hispanic middle school in the Washington D.C. area where I was introducing the kids to ice skating. Shortly after sharing the joys of ice skating with the class, I heard the words, which rang so familiarly in my ear, "Black kids don't ice skate." Those words took me back to when I was fourteen and was so excited to tell my classmates about my love for ice skating. This time, I was able to share with the class some of the Black and Brown skating legends and current minority figure skating stars, who they'd never heard of or seen before my introduction. I was so glad that I was given the opportunity to instill knowledge about what was possible for minorities in the sport, but saddened to realize the stereotypes haven't changed. It became clear to me that there is more that we can do to highlight the success of minorities in figure skating.

Hearing these perceptions from these kids has been the fuel to my fire in my coaching, as well. Today, I coach at over three rinks in the District, Maryland, Virginia (D.M.V.) area. Many of my students are skaters of color and I try to spread my love of skating through lessons and motivational speaking. One of my students mentioned to me how refreshing it is to have a coach who looks like him, which makes it easier and exciting to come to the rink and train each day. In addition, I have worked on collaborating with minority coaches and their students through initiatives under the Diversify Ice foundation.

From my experience, the disparity of race in figure skating comes from both ends of the spectrum—top-down inattention to the issues of race from skating governance and bottom-up socio-economic issues that affect how Black and Brown families depict and associate themselves with the sport. This feedback loop perpetuates the racially homogenous nature of the sport where neither side truly makes an effort to be associated with each other. However, there are things that can be done to help move this sport in a direction that will foster a more diverse figure skating community.

Things the Figure Skating Governance can do:

Today, out of the eighteen board members on the U.S. Figure Skating Association Board of Directors, none of them are

African American. With this disparity in the board members, it is unlikely that the issues of race for Black and Brown kids in figure skating will be a priority.

There are opportunities for U.S figure skating to develop dedicated diversity and inclusion resources for elite minority athletes, as some of their challenges are very different than other skaters. What's more, the continued involvement of skaters of color also have a shorter lifespan.

U.S. Figure Skating has done a great job in supporting *introductory and recreational* programs for minority skaters through programs like the Prudential Skating Fund Gift. Some of the recipients from these types of programs include Figure Skating in Harlem and the Fort Dupont Ice Arena. The Figure Skating in Harlem highlights in their mission that they are an organization for girls of color that combines the power of education with access to the artistic discipline of figure skating to build champions in life (figureskatinginharlem.org). This is an incredible program that provides introduction to aspects of skating and academic enrichment opportunities for minority girls in New York. In addition, the Fort Dupont Ice Arena highlights on their website their mission to provide increased opportunity, education, and inspiration to the young people of Washington, D.C. and the surrounding area through ice skating and educational activities (FDIA.org). They provide subsidized figure skating, hockey and speed skating lessons to youth in Washington D.C.

These great introductory skating programs, however, are based on recreational and initial exposure for minorities to simply get basic participation in the sport. They do not foster *elite competitive* minority athletes for success in the sport. Diversify Ice Foundation wants to bridge the gap for programs like these, to enable talented minority figure skaters who want to achieve their fullest potential at the elite competitive levels. Diversify Ice Fellowship and Foundation is the first foundation aiming to support minority figure skaters Nationwide in their elite competitive goals. This foundation aims to provide financial support, resources, and community needed for minorities to be successful in competitive figure skating.

Getting this foundation off the ground wasn't easy and we have expressed interest to partner with figure skating governance and their grant opportunities to support more minorities at the elite levels. We have also worked with local businesses that share our vision. Diversify Ice Foundation took polls, interviewed minority skaters about their needs, and created our own networks and events to support minority skaters nationwide. We hope that the public and U.S. figure skating can make use of our data and take lessons learned around race in this sport. Diversify Ice foundation welcomes partnerships that will strengthen diversity at elite levels of figure skating.

There's so much information about figure skating online and it can be difficult for new skaters and their families to know which direction they should take. The figure skating governing bodies can help provide transparency on the tracks and trajectories that skaters can choose between for competitive and recreational skating. Sadly, there are many instances where skaters chose the wrong membership path for their goals. For example, I learned of skaters who took the Ice Skating Institute (ISI) testing and competition track for several years, which is geared for recreational skating, with the hopes and intention of qualifying for the Olympics and other Team USA international events. Only to learn later that they should have been on the U.S. Figure Skating membership track. These skaters have wasted endless hours and money on the wrong track for their goals. Many skaters, several of them being skaters of color, have decided to leave the sport because of the lack of transparency, and wasted hours and money.

Furthermore, there are significant costs associated with figure skating. In addition to the cost of skates, blade sharpening, coaching fees, ice time, and more, figure skating membership costs are also a huge barrier. In order for figure skaters to compete at the qualifying levels that can lead to U.S. Nationals and Team USA events, figure skaters must be part of U.S. Figure Skating and part of a figure skating club or pay an individual membership fee with no club affiliation for around $144/ yearly. On the USFSA website, U.S. Figure Skating has shared that all local clubs and programs set their own membership dues. However, these membership costs can be greater than one hundred dollars. These costs alone can be a deterrent for skaters and their families, who want to figure skate competitively, when they can play basketball or football for free at their schools or local community centers.

Figure Skating Costs *Analysis and research collected from Diversify Ice Foundation		
	Cost	Average Replacement
Figure Skating Boots *Does not includes blades	$800- $1200	8 months to 12 months
Figure Skating Blades *Blades and boots are sold separately for high end competitive skating	$500-$1000	12 -24 months
Blade Sharpening	$20	3 weeks
Freestyle (Advanced training sessions) At least 3 sessions a day 5 days a	$10- $15 per session $30-45 per	

week	day $7800-$11700 yearly	
Coaching lessons (Minimum 3 days a week)	$50-$100/ hourly	Year-round
Costumes (1 for short &1 for long) 2 costumes per season	$100-$2000	Yearly or every 2 years
Annual Skating Membership	$100+	
Figure Skating Tests 1. Pre-Preliminary (Moves/ Free) 2. Preliminary (Moves/ Free) 3. Pre-Juvenile (Moves/ Free) 4. Juvenile (Moves/ Free) 5. Intermediate (Moves/ Free) 6. Novice (Moves/ Free) 7. Junior (Moves/ Free)	Moves in the field test total, if skater passes all of the levels on the first try can cost over $400 Skaters may also pay nearly $400 to complete the Free	Skaters tend to advance to the next level every year or every other year. In order to advance to each level, skaters must take the test for that level.

8. Senior (Moves/ Free) Cost of moves in the field test range from $40 at the lowest levels to $75 at the Senior levels.	Skating tests over their training career.	
Competitions Event registration fee Coaches fees	Usually ranges from $40+100 Plus pay an additional cost for any additional event	Skaters usually complete around 3 preseason events a year.

While skating costs are expensive, The U.S. Figure Skating

Association does offer athlete funding opportunities to U.S. Team

envelope A, B and C athletes by assisting them with their skating

expenses (USFSA.org). Criteria to be selected for these envelope

tiers are based on skater's placement on national and international

events. If selected for international events, the skater can win prize

money if they medal. There are other additional financial aid

opportunities to support elite level skaters, such as the Memorial

Fund. The Memorial Fund Awards are based on financial need and competitive history (USFSA.org).

Retention in figure skating is also an issue for skaters of color. Many skaters of color who train competitively do not stay in the sport because there are limited opportunities for skaters of color to be a successful athletically and professionally. Skaters of color who decide to transition into coaching are likely not to have as many students as their equivalent who is not a minority. The majority of skaters who want to participate in skating are not black or brown, so they will likely not pick a minority coach.

Again, skaters of color are rarely televised, so new skaters, even skaters of color, may not even consider taking lessons from a coach of color because they may believe that a minority coach may not have as much experience, background, or political capital to help skaters achieve their dreams. The latter, political capital, is important in this sport considering the politics that's ingrained at every level of figure skating. Some examples of where you can see politics in the sport is in the judging, selection of skaters to international events (International competition selection based more on subjective body of work than final placement at Nationals), show performance opportunities, and coaching opportunities at rinks. Given the low probability of students, it is not enticing for coaches of color to pay the huge costs to be a coach.

The cost for coaches to be compliant, legally allowed to coach, can run several hundred dollars a year. Cost includes: U.S. figure skating membership, Safesport ® online Training, background checks, coach education requirement, liability insurance, and Professional Skaters Association (PSA). While many of these trainings prove to be valuable, the costs remain a barrier for potential elite minority coaches because there is little to no return on investment. In addition, coaching contracts are often set up with the rinks requiring commission to be paid from the coach to the rink per lesson.

The educational pathways for skaters are often limited in comparison to sports like football and basketball, where scholarships are abundant. College scholarships for figure skating are very rare and the amount is extremely limited. Often, skaters who choose a competitive figure skating track are often home schooled or does partial school days to make time for prime training facility hours, which can make it difficult to be as academically competitive. However, skaters that are successful at the international level, usually attract some of the best schools in the country. Families that do not come from means, may find that the financial sacrifices they made in their skating career limits their ability to take additional investments in their academics, such as school loans. In contrast, sports like football and basketball have low family financial burdens, but can yield full academic scholarships and a successful career in leagues such as the National Basketball Association (NBA) or National Football League.

Figure skating governance can find creative ways to partner with universities to offer opportunities and scholarships to former figure skaters who want to build a career in figure skating and also develop pathways to success for life after figure skating. In addition, finding ways to cut costs on coaching compliance or provide supplemental support to minority coaches would help attract diversity in figure skating coaching at an elite level.

<u>What the Community can do:</u>

Local businesses and schools can seek out opportunities to partner with ice rinks. I would have never had a chance to try skating if it wasn't for my middle school providing me with the opportunity through partnerships with a local ice rink. Schools should also consider introducing figure skating as part of their physical education (P.E.) requirement. Some private schools and non-minority public schools provide skating and hockey opportunities to their students. Unfortunately, low-income schools, that are comprised mostly of minorities, do not have these partnerships and opportunities to be exposed to ice skating. Figure skating governance can set up grants directly with low-income minority schools to provide these opportunities more broadly.

Joel coaches ice skating to a group of kids

What Black and Brown families can do:

Black and Brown kids often do not want to try competitive skating because they are not visually represented in the sport, unlike basketball and football. However, families should encourage their kids to try a different type of sport, such as ice skating because it has many of the athletic qualities that attract minorities to sports like basketball, track and field, and football.

For example, in basketball, in order to dunk the ball successfully at

the ten-foot-high hoop, the player must gather speed and jump up

high, while maintaining balance. This progression of gathering

speed to jump is very similar to figure skating jumps. Skaters have

to gather speed by skating fast and then jump up high, in order to

complete one to four rotations in the air, while keeping their

balance. In fact, basketball stars, such as Michael Jordan and

Dwyane Wade have made popular the 360 dunk, requiring the

player to jump and spin in the air a full rotation while completing

the dunk in the hoop.

Lebron James jumps up for a basketball dunk. Photo by Christopher Powers (Yahoo Finance)

Emmanuel Savary jumps up for a quadruple jump Photo by Joel Savary

While figure skating is not a contact sport, unlike football, there are similarities in what is needed to be successful in both. Football requires a lot of aerobic endurance, speed, balance, flexibility, and technique. If any of you have been tackled on the football field, that impact can be likened to a figure skater falling from a four revolution jump three feet in the air. However, if you prefer contact sports, such as football, you may want to consider trying ice hockey. While you won't be running with a football in your hand, you will be traveling twice as fast on ice to score the hockey puck into the goal. To be good at hockey, a basic skill of ice skating is needed.

For kids that enjoy running track and field, they may consider speed skating. In fact, speed skating has started to see some growth in popularity among the black and brown communities. In the 2006 Winter Olympics, speed skater Shani

Davis became the first black athlete to win a gold medal in an individual event at the Olympic Winter games. Speed skating and ice hockey has a greater likelihood of attracting minorities because they are not based on subjective judging like figure skating. However, figure skating, speed skating, and hockey all require the foundation of learning ice skating.

Maame Biney became the first African American woman to qualify for the speed skating team (Inside Edition: Getty)

Michael Johnson at the 1996 Olympics. Photo taken by Gary M. Prior / Getty Images

We can also make comparisons to many other sports that are popular in the black and brown communities. Recognizing and demonstrating the similarities of ice skating and many of the popular sports that minority kids enjoy is important to bridge the gap with kids. Diversify Ice has done work with minority skaters in bridging the gap with other sports and popular activities to encourage minority kids and their families to get on the ice and skate.

One of the big issues, as I learned very quickly in grade school, is the perception that figure skating is perceived as an effeminate activity for many people of color. The views of these kids, who are now adults, are probably the same and they would have likely passed down these views to their kids and social networks. There is an obvious contrast from the grace required in skating from that of the aggressiveness required to tackle someone in football.

Masculinity is taken very seriously in Black culture and anything that may appear to deviate is not usually accepted. The reinforcement of music choices in figure skating that are lyrical and classical in nature being tied to this sport may not reflect masculinity for many boys of color. Unfortunately, these classical and lyrical music choices are reinforced by judges to demonstrate a serious and artistic skater. Instead, creating an environment where alternative music and styles, including music genre choices from the African diaspora, can be accepted as serious skating music would help the image of figure skating in America. Of course, conservative judges and skaters may counter that new and alternative music types won't translate internationally. However, I believe it can and will overtime, if these changes are first accepted domestically.

ROAD TO DIVERSITY

Figure skating in America has done a great job of keeping the status quo, while continued reforms are needed. Although there have been incremental improvements with judging transparency, and increased competitiveness (with minimal IJS scores to qualify for nationals), there is still so much more that needs to be done. This book has shed some light on some of the more pervasive racial issues in figure skating that all of us, despite our background, can help change. What's more, I hope it can be referenced as a roadmap to help skaters and their families effectively navigate the complex and political figure skating ecosystem, especially minorities who want to figure skate at an elite level. In addition, I hope it challenges the preconceived notions around what activities Black and Brown kids should and could do.

It is my goal that figure skating will progress to a point where the U.S. National competitors are reflective of what a diverse America looks like. In time, it would be great to say that America has produced more skaters of color at the international level. Finally, I hope this book will at least be a conversation starter of where we are with race in sports, because it is only a microcosm and reflection of where we currently stand with race in America.

I have included a path to diversity checklist, so that we can measure the progress of diversity over the years in figure skating. I believe that the milestones in this checklist will start the conversation that will spark changes when it comes to diversity in

figure skating.

Paths to Diversity in Figure Skating Checklist	
U.S Figure Skating	
☐ Add people of color on USFSA governance board	
☐ Develop or partner with funding opportunities dedicated to elite/ developing skaters of color	
☐ Showcase more **elite** skaters of color in USFSA televised publicity	
☐ Lower the barrier of entry cost to competitive figure skating	
☐ Lower the barrier of entry compliance cost to coaching figure skating	
☐ Provide a pathway for skaters to transition from competitive skating to college/ universities with partnerships	
☐ Encourage Diversity in the qualifying judging panels	
People of Color	
☐ Parents should encourage children to participate in unconventional sports such as ice skating/ hockey	
☐ Challenge preconceived notions around boys participating in ice skating	
☐ Provide support and challenge preconceived notions around people of color ice skating.	
Diversify Ice Foundation	

☐ Develop opportunities to showcase skaters of color	
☐ Provide an outlet for equipment donations for skaters	
☐ Provide opportunity for skaters of color to acquire sponsorship	
☐ Provide a network of minority figure skaters and coaches	
☐ Provide greater funding support for minority skaters, limited resources	
☐ Provide support for minorities to participate in judging and coaching.	
☐ Collaborate with groups, such as Figure Skating in Harlem to provide pathways to elite competitive skating.	
Ice Rinks	
☐ Provide skating sessions that celebrate black history or diversity	
☐ Provide free/ reduced price public session opportunities to low income and minority schools	
☐ Invest in the development of more rinks in minority neighborhoods	
Coaches	
☐ Connect minority skaters to the local community of minority coaches	
☐ Pass down lessons learned from minority skaters to help other skaters	

"Power is not given to you. You have to take it."

– Beyonce

Chapter 9
Parting Words

Skating is an amazing sport that innately teaches life lessons through its training and mastering of even the most basic of skating skills. For example, the more cliché metaphors of skating teach us that when we fall on the ice, as in life, we need to get back up and try again. However, we should take these platitudes of life a step further. When the world tells you that you cannot do something because of how you look, where you come from, or your economic background, find a path forward to achieve your vision. To add to that, do not let the systems of the world force you to conform to something you are not in order to promise you success. I believe the most valuable gift you can contribute to the sport, and to anything you do in life, is being yourself.

What I have learned from my skating career and even my professional career as in life, you may be in venues where you are the only one who looks like you. You may be the only male skater on the ice, the only person of color at your job, or the only person in your class who does not come from a family of financial means. However, these differences do not make you less than anyone else and shouldn't deter you from being confident in who you are, and in your abilities, to make a positive statement in the room.

When it comes to diversity, the role a minority plays as a participant is often much greater than themselves. A minority skaters' participation in the sport may open the door to more minorities being inspired to be like you and follow in your footsteps. When I began skating, my younger brother looked up to me, realizing that being a black male skater is possible, and he decided that he wanted to skate too. In this case, I was a role model for my brother, as he has been for many other minorities who told me they started skating from seeing him skate. That visible connection is critically important to create a feedback loop of future minority participation. So, I urge skaters of color not give up in this sport simply because of the racial disparities, discrimination, or instances of microaggression, as you may be inspiring someone else just from your presence on the ice.

The path to diversity in skating will not be an easy one, but it is possible. The barriers are multifaceted, and its painful history is pervasive. However, all things must evolve, including ice skating, in order to survive. In recent years, we are seeing a surge of diversity in a number of sports that had a history of being predominantly monochromatic. However, achieving diversity in this sport is a job for each and every one of us, despite our position, racial background, and social class. I am optimistic that the future of skating will improve, so that all people, regardless of their background, will be able to enjoy this sport at the recreational and elite training levels.

Highlights of Issues

- **Cultural differences**
    - NFL: 65% Black
    - NBA 75% black
    - Skating not integrated as a recreational sport for minorities
- **Absence of racial ties**
    - 1988 was the only year a skater of color was sent to the Worlds/ Olympics
    - No role model to look up to in the sport for minorities
    - 2/18 (11%) women of color represented at nationals
    - 1/20 (5%) Men of color represented at nationals

- o 3/63 (4%) total Athlete Teams of color at the senior level
- **Opaque Judging System**
  - o Judging system- Is it fair?
    - Artistic mark very subjective, technical scores are less subjective
  - o Coaches student relationship
    - Skaters of color
  - o Minorities may prefer more objectively scored sports for fear of racial bias.
    - Score the most points
    - Reaches finish line fastest
- **Lack of socio-economic resources**
  - o Rinks primarily located in white affluent neighborhoods
  - o Scholarships programs limited or unavailable
  - o Expenses of Equipment, coaching, travel
  - o No pathways of success after skating
- **Skating Governance**
  - o No board of directors of color
  - o No programs developed to address racial disparities in competitive figure skaters of color

References

Boyalan-Pett, Liam. "20 Years ago, Michael Johnson Set a New Gold Standard for speed." Image retrieved from https://www.sbnation.com/2016/7/20/12212298/michael-johnson-200-meter-record-gold-cleats-olympics-usa

Brown, Sherronda. "How defiant Black women athletes like Surya Bonaly and Serena Williams inspire me and help lay the groundwork for the future." April 4, 2019. Photo retrieved from http://blackyouthproject.com/how-defiant-black-women-athletes-like-surya-bonaly-and-serena-williams-inspire-me-and-help-lay-the-groundwork-for-the-future/

Dunn, Amina. "Younger, college-educated black Americans are most likely to feel need to 'code-switch" Code-switch. 2019. In *PewResearch.org.* Retrieved October 8, 2018, from https://www.pewresearch.org/fact-tank/2019/09/24/younger-college-educated-black-americans-are-most-likely-to-feel-need-to-code-switch/

"Dupont Ice Arena Website: Our Mission." Fort Dupont Ice Arena. Retrieved March 19, 2019, from https://www.fdia.org/about-us/

"Figure Skating in Harlem: Our Story." The Figure Skating in Harlem. Retrieved March 19, 2019, from https://figureskatinginharlem.org/our-story/

Gavilanes, Nancy. Jan 14 2001. *FIGURE SKATING; A Pioneer at the Rink Is Proud of Her Legacy.* Retrieved from https://www.nytimes.com/2001/01/14/sports/figure-skating-a-pioneer-at-the-rink-is-proud-of-her-legacy.html

Hastings, Deborah. "Winter Olympics: Who is Speed Skater Maame Biney?" Image retrieved from https://www.insideedition.com/winter-olympics-who-speed-skater-maame-biney-40563.

Howard, Johnette. *"OVER EASY FOR SURYA BONALY THE SKATING HAS NEVER BEEN THE HARD PART."* March 6, 1995. Retrieved from https://www.si.com/vault/1995/03/06/8092675/over-easy-for-surya-bonaly-the-skating-has-never-been-the-hard-part

LUTZ, RACHEL. DANIEL JANIN/AFP/GETTY IMAGES, DAVID MADISON/GETTY IMAGES / NBC OLYMPICS. "1988: Katarina Witt wins her second Olympic gold in thrilling 'Battle of the Carmens'." February 6, 2018. Image retrieved from http://archivepyc.nbcolympics.com/news/1988-katarina-witt-wins-her-second-olympic-gold-thrilling-battle-carmens

Mathewson, Eryn. "Former Olympian Surya Bonaly says don't call her a rebel, call her fearless. David Madison of Getty Image. Image Retrieved from https://theundefeated.com/features/former-olympian-surya-bonaly-says-dont-call-her-a-rebel-call-her-fearless/

Powers, Christopher. "LeBron James recreates vintage dunk against Suns, continues to age like a fine wine." *Yahoo Finance*, Image retrieved from https://finance.yahoo.com/news/lebron-james-recreates-vintage-dunk-141400057.html

Reed, Christopher. Mabel Fairbanks: Figure skater kept out of the Olympics by racism. Mon 8 Oct 2001. Retrieved October 8, 2018 from https://www.theguardian.com/news/2001/oct/08/guardianobituaries

Uchenna Edeh "Mabel Fairbanks: Pioneer African American Figure Skater." November 14, 2015. Image retrieved from https://kentakepage.com/mabel-fairbanks-pioneer-african-american-figure-skater/

"2018-2019 U.S Figure Skating Fact Sheet." U.S. Figure Skating. Retrieved October 8, 2018, from https://www.usfsa.org/content/FactSheet.pdf

Made in the USA
Monee, IL
16 February 2020